Endorsements for *Clean*

The inimitable SPM's first full-length collection is a fear-and-loathing-journey-book through addiction and back again. These are beautifully written, harrowing, wise, tightly-wound poems of witness, survival and hard-won insight. There is a wry playfulness and joy here too, and sex, and a deep engagement with cultural touchstones (including the Rocky Horror Picture Show). Above all, there is an understanding of the true cost of everything: *remember,/ getting clean is a form of grief / so let go / of your own ghost: / a wake, every day.*

MELINDA SMITH

After years of watching SPM perform across stages, their poems achieve new volume on the page. Split into the three sections of an elegy, this debut collection performs an act of resurrection; the dead do not stay dead in these poems of addiction and obsession. Even within a landscape of hurt, these stories form a forest of love so wisely woven that the reader can take shelter in its shade.

Despite what the title may suggest, this collection is still on its knees scrubbing at memories. In Scott-Patrick Mitchell's poetry 'Clean' is not a destination; it is a grief still wailing, a queer body undergoing renovation, it is the whispered promise of daybreak.

MADDIE GODFREY

When ghosts are buried and burned new rituals glisten. *Clean* cuts through crystal hollows of addiction, tracing sockets of trauma to the lucent clearing where the poem is being. A blazing collection of aches and the words needed to mend them.

TAMRYN BENNETT

This work will change readers – it will reach deep into their psyches and have them checking their interior lives, as well as how they live their lives in the shared world. Scott-Patrick Mitchell is a remarkable poet who shifts and realigns language, because it must be placed under pressure, given the pressures we live under. Confronting the trauma of addiction, we move with the poet through to being 'clean', and all the complexities around that new clarity. A poet of intense empathy with others, who has a unique way of processing ideas that arise from experience, they travel the streets of Perth, and the contradictions of private grief and communal presence, with phenomenal linguistic skill. This is the book that comes after and beyond Michael Dransfield's *Drug Poems*. It is a lodestar book – a book you will never forget.

JOHN KINSELLA

Scott Patrick-Mitchell's poems will mark you, the way desire lines wear their maps into the soft places of a city. He makes you look, intimately and generously at spaces it would be far easier to turn away from, by meticulously crafting hard subject matter into exquisitely musical language.

AMANDA JOY

Clean

Scott-Patrick Mitchell

Scott-Patrick Mitchell is a WA-based non-binary poet who is a guest on unceded Whadjuk Noongar land. SPM's work appears in *Contemporary Australian Poetry*, *The Fremantle Press Anthology of Western Australian Poetry*, *Solid Air*, *Stories of Perth* and *Going Postal*. They have a number of previous chapbooks, including *songs for the ordinary mass* (PressPress, 2009) and *The Rutting Season* (Mulla Mulla Press, 2012).

A seasoned performance poet, Mitchell has toured Australia with works that have fused language and minimal baroque to the 2015 one-person showcase *THE 24 HOUR PERFORMANCE POEM*. SPM has won Coal Creek's Literary Award for Poetry, Melbourne Poets Union's Martin Downey Urban Realist Poetry Award and The Wollongong Short Story Prize. A focus for the poet is in building community through their work with Perth Poetry Festival and WA Poets Inc's Emerging Writers Program. They live with two black cats, Beowulf and Bones.

The author would like to acknowledge the Traditional Custodians of this region on which these poems were written and all First Nations across this continent. Sovereignty was never ceded. They pay respect to Elders past, and present. Always was, always is and always will be Aboriginal Land.

Scott-Patrick Mitchell

Clean

UPSWELL

First published in Australia in 2022
Reprinted in 2023
by Upswell Publishing
Perth, Western Australia
upswellpublishing.com

ISBN: 978-0-6452479-3-0

A catalogue record for this book is available from the National Library of Australia

Cover artwork: Penny Coss, Wrapped Up in a Magellan Cloud, 2019
Cover design by Chil3
Typeset in Foundry Origin by Lasertype
Printed by McPherson's Printing Group

for the emergency workers, for the families, for the friends
for those lost & for those who found themselves again

for my mum & my sisters
thank you

Contents

DIRTY

Addiction is a quiet mouth
and it doesn't care who it swallows.

– Bill Moran, *Dear Amy*

The Mourning Star

The victimization of children is nowhere forbidden;
what is forbidden is to write about it.

– Alice Miller

i.

The first star pierces
with dead light.

Is a dirge.
Is you.

Is known by how it tugs,
draws into. Sight shall fill
with shapes.

How we monster a bed.

ii.

You are an ecological disaster.
All your teeth are falling out.
Because you refuse to speak,
to shout. You fill your veins
with swamp. Let your anger
be the climate, raging.

Become sea flood. Salt yourself.

Let crystals sting as you rub them
into your skin.

iii.

There is a man who claims to be family.
He teaches you to whimper with a full mouth.
He will lay his hands across naked sheets.

A stain remains.

As does ink.

iv.

Night was created so the gods had somewhere to hide:
their sins; their sins; their sins. And us, made
in their image – minus wing or cloven hoof – we follow suit.

v.

At midnight,
gather all your teeth

and bury them.

At a crossroads.
In a cauldron.
In a coffin.

vi.

That first star:
it can do nothing to save us
from ourselves,
from those men,
all ivory and ache.

The first star weeps.

Because to bear witness is a burden.

And we cannot sleep.

Leave your body:
as ghost
step into atramentous.

This Town

This town is packed with fits and pipedreams, cracking. Here, the kids are addicts. Their folks too. In alleyways, syringes scab. Beer bottles vulgar the park. Sun churns bitumen as we burn from the inside out. Funny how this drug is anything but chill. A storm rolls into the curtains, threatening to arrive. But it never does. At least, not in the sky. Black abyss eyes. You can tell the quality by the way some townsfolk behave: when the gear is good, they fight; when the gear is cut, burglaries go up. Then there are those who howl the night, half-naked, wrapped in winter's thrill. And each other. The cops are all exhausted. It's not just them. Those who don't use barricade bars across windows, unlock cars for fear of cleaning up more shattered glass. Black abyss eyes eye you off. How a snatched bag can fly. Those two days before Centrelink are bliss: tension dissolves into sprinkler's hiss. Summer heat induces sleep. Then they all powder keg their heads, again. Vicious dogs. More vicious cycles. More black eyes. After the third B&E, Mr Patterson, he'd had enough: took a shotgun, blew up at some dealer's house. Two dead. That night, at the pub, he was heralded a hero. The beer gunpowdered similar plots. A week later, the bikies moved in. Vigilantes quit the job before they even took it up. Mr P, he's now serving life. So are we. The cops are still exhausted. Nobody can sell up and cash-grab, especially when you live four doors down from a meth lab. We learn to staunch as the kids become thinner and rabid.

The Stanzas of Shabu

Shabu is a slang term for methamphetamine in Japan and SE Asia.

snow-goose shards
sky flecked white:
Shabu is high tonight

–

Shabu freezes pipe:
inhale mind-blow
of ice, crystal, snow

–

in mirror, Shabu –
thin white girl wants you
to eat something

–

Shabu changes hands
lays down: on mirror, CD case, in spoon
wearing dynamic diamond gown

–

Shabu, wrapped in plastic,
as twisted as she is Lynchian

–

crushed Shabu
spreads herself
cartilage thin

–

Shabu smoking
is a dream, cracked
from overuse: black satin

–

¿day seven?
yes, Shabu,
day seven

–

shut up
Shabu
shut up

–

Shabu vomits in anticipation:
what is an addict?

–

Shabu
now we sleep?

no, she answers
          now more
          we seek

him

out farther, stars are the
art in heaven. hollow be the

sky that does not contain
them. hello be the aim of

an introduction. twine
winged one, my heart is

undone. you are worth every
penny from above. give in

& say let us go to bed
for we need to undress

for we need to undress
& press us against us.

it will lead us to
temptation, which will

quiver an upheaval. for
i am your winged one

& our love will flower
song in the face of the

eternal. forever
endeavour to be a

lover, a partner, a boy,
a man.

the blood thieves

when we were gone
we were an ache of poison

grey thin wind
erosion

we wanted to steal
red

rush of blood
from their heads

make their health ours
dab desire

pinch capillaries
a rouge rogue

lifting to the skin
paint borders

beyond our own

It Begins With Burning (An Obituary)

I taste tobacco on your lips: rum-soaked ash, calling. For an ex-smoker, this kiss is dangerous. You make me start again. Turn my breath to smoke. I learn your perfection in rolling a cigarette with hands too small to hold the volume of my lungs. My smokes are crooked, jag yellow stains across fingers. Nicotine, a residual. There is a build-up inside me too: for you. In bed, we are opposites. My palms are as confident as rollie papers succumbing to spit. Yours shake, as if desperate to ignite. You fumble to keep a match like me. It takes you a month to learn how to make me burn. I discover your firebreaks in a matter of days, leap over them, reduce you to embers. We are Pyrocene. We are lovers made from bushfire, pouring ourselves on to the other. Kindling. We set off fire alarms. A sky smudged with smoke: the window blushes sunset.

Anti-Pastoral

Gather holes. Pierce landscape's fold. Bleed toward surface. We divine entry into poem, journey wreckage up an arm. Below stone, an arterial flow. Spectral, earth lifts. Ghost plume, bloody ectoplasm, like a séance. The medium is far from normal. This is illicit. Vomit slow capture release, chant so only the dead can hear: bring hollow inside self. Fire stolen from dreams, burn. In our beings, we bury it. Deeper. This is arson from within. Begin bubbling. An exchange occurs. As parrots, we mimic how the other rides current. We feather relentlessly against the imaginary wind that gathers at the sleeve of this scarp. Purple swells in pointillism. Habitually, we dig and watch sand sear into glass as lightning strikes & strikes a path. We grow fulgurite art. Window ground is a revelation: here is the track addiction carves. Needlecraft a map of becoming lost. As survivors on this road, we are constantly crashing. You wish we were snakes shucking skin, how this heat swallows everything, fades meat from pink to grey to gone. White ache of salted world. At night, this desert is frozen. We are left wandering.

Night Orchids

i.

Our lucent teeth spark the rainbow dark.
Here, we do not use words like *love*.
Instead, we speak with hands that hold
as shoulders tussle
the roughhouse rougher.

In the absence of daylight,
we are just two young men,
silent save for giggle and shoe scuff:

we do not rouse suspicion when touching.

ii.

In the park we whisper *sanctuary*.

In the dark, we kiss, disturb crickets.

Moon pours itself into oval stygian pitch,
latches to hair, brings blonde to brim
as if stars are contained within:
an equation curls from out your scalp.

You fall onto, and into, my tongue.

Beneath clothes, your alabaster muscles
harden my palms.

iii.

As if summoned to speak
a benediction of sprinkler:
the grass opens.

Lift.

Water arcs, a spray
and hiss as we grip.

Bearing down, the bore
empties over us.

We allow ourselves to pull the other
into the other, wetter. We laugh.
Then we dance. Across the road,
house lights flicker, cause curtains to twitch.

We ignore them.

iv.

Who knew running would be our rhythm.

Our feet squelch, pavement slaps
we whoop from out the stoop
of our mouths.

Us, kids, wrapped in nebulous time.

And there, in the middle of the street,
halogen inside the other's eyes, we kiss.

Again.

Here, we glisten, sacred.
World bows:
if this were a poem
wildflowers would luminescent
road into ribbon,
tied around us.

As dawn encroaches
we do not unfold
our bush orchid hold.

necking

he asks me to do him up again
reclined like Jesus Christ died
head to toe, a crown of thorns
tightening inside.

i ride like Mary Magdalene
summoned to administer to his sores
wet with swab & holy words
cooed & purred

are you sure?

nodding, he rolls his eyes into
self, as though meditating.

                                        i

                                            exhale

steady   myself

count to three, then go
straight for the jugular.

                                    phlebotomy is an
art that requires extending sense & feel,
syringing tip to touch plasma's bed,
arteries artfully penetrated.

                                    in the rush
his world collapses outward & his
eyes blacken into holes of deceit &
greed.

                                    each time we do this
he pronounces every name in the world
in one single breath as if speaking creation,

a communion with ancient gods, holy & dead,
precise with precision & habitual revision:

this is how i know i've done a good job.

Icarus Finds A Lover in The Afterlife

feathering i fall
                    featherward

                              , toward
        fountain he pours from
        purr in his throat, hymn
                                        sleep

                                   . in the fold of moonlight, handheld & elbowed
                          , he guides me
                                             , sleepy dreamhead fledging in bed

   . i snore, adore spooning his strength to make
      believe we are meandering beings tethered in dreams

                                                    . our clasp
      grasps beneath the cushions pillowing our night
            . here, i hide an egg tooth, made for coining a new one
            : i want him to grow inside my mouth as i articulate flight

            . if i can't have that, then give my beak dawn choral, evensong

                    . from bone, grow shards
                                        birds use to migrate & thrive

                                             . together, we search for home
                                        on wings made from z's
                          . together, we sky roam lunar high, melt with sigh &
                          murmuring

Homebake

Hell is the wait. But here is the strange thing – how this unnatural time, this time that exists only in anticipation of another time, can become something pure. We become junkies of the wait...

John Kinsella & McKenzie Wark

All good things run out: into traffic; of steam; away from you. When they do – when we are left with a gram bag, crystal clear – we have a plan in place: our washbags launder dirt in them. This solution is neither beautiful nor holy, but it's the only faith we have. We set aside all points, from those that missed the mark to those that did the job. They are back-up in our moments of drought. How we thirst, itch toward midnight. Nobody's answered their phone. She digs out Pyrex. In the hours without, we bake. Dime bags dined from are cut into pieces, soaked, water stained with meth retained. This is neither beautiful nor holy, but oh so necessary. Prayers chew our tongues. Strained, conversation is minimal, a slow heat meditating between us as we boil remnants: silence bubbles the house. We reduce what's left. In the hours that simmer, we clean: her on her hands and knees while I climb the walls, a sugar soap bleach removing every mark scuffing up our world. Our elbow grease is a resolve. The clocks are cottonmouth. Try not to scratch. Finally, the zen rakes an un-white dust. A substitute emerges across Pyrex. We sit down to dine at 4 a.m., hungry to see what we have summoned. The colour is never becoming: brown is a dredge is a dirge. We filter out the green and yellow sound and stick it to ourselves to keep going. Because that's what addicts do. What comes next is neither beautiful nor holy. But sometimes it is brighter than the dawn, saintly: if we are lucky, the day will begin, early, high on chatter and exhilarating thoughts. Our points become bigger than the first time we made them. But there are times when the whole ritual is for nothing: broken, faith must beg for a miracle. So we pray someone will credit our roll... even if it means we have to wait some more.

whipping boy

how, in school, fights had different rules:
you got punched, you hit the ground.

but I was dogged, determined,
friends screaming *stay down*.

I never listened.

now, when they bash you,
you wish you were see-through.

but you ain't.

swelling shall appear
here, here &   there.

sinking in, turn violet from ultra-violence.

when casting roles we are never told
you: you shall play the victim.

& you: you shall be the boy
made just for whipping.

catch yourself before you fade.

this is not a love song for their baseball bats,
the way they laugh with every swing, every
whack.

this is not a love song for the petrol they pour
on me, nor the lighter that refuses to catch.

this is a love song for the voice in my head
who says *now is not the time to play dead.*

in the distance, sirens wail assistance.

Co-Dependency (How Terror Forms)

i.

Repetition is a bruise thing.
Bodies are built for enduring.

We get ripped off, pick at scars,
slide ice into dry reservoir.

Blood thick with dehydration.

Median cubital vein, darken.

We are obsessed by how a crystal can burn:
the skin; our cash; these teeth are caving in.

How we bleed, visibly.

If only we could weep.

ii.

We hock our dignity
again.

This is a ritual:
each time
the veins
in our arms
collapse
some more.

We become a multiplicity,
frothing at the mouth.

A laceration of days
carving buccal mucosa:

tongue invisible stutter
of ridge & contour.

iii.

We buy our capital back.

Then we drudge,
walk blocks
as pilgrimage.

When a dealer
returns our call,
we shall fall
on spears:

this, our worship.

We burn
ourselves alive
from the inside.

My face has become
scree, disfigured by
detachment.

Yours has too:
I count the bones
behind your ears.

But still we chase the glacial
travel night by the star charts
that track marks up our arms.

the hoarding

acquisition is habit-driven:
we lose ourselves in the collections
we let consume our shelves.

if beginning is to summon
liberation comes through discarding:
to give up is to let go
& we have so far to go.

but first we must accumulate
like the heady rush of fresh verge diving lust
the night untouched by anyone else:
rubbish people set out for us.

we are wet with anticipatory sweat
as we weave streets unknown
excited at mounds of potential.

this is a shared expedition
of roadsides as fields
ripe with harvest
wheat & meal.

the eucalypts lean in.

a gathering begins:
we are firestorm
inflamed mouths of ember & smoke.
as kindling we envelop: books; letters;
strange ligaments from appliances;
a cartilage of former selves.

at some point, hoardings will break
& the mass we amass
shall infiltrate day
as a seething takes place:
nothing is ever contained.

we clamber.
objects pile around us:
suffocation sinks in.

to let go of all this we must
let go of useless things.

we are breaking up.

inner pity poems

after John Kinsella's ***Globe Hotel and Inner City Poems***

i.

our gravity has no centre:
abstract where we belong.
become invisible, one of many.
satellite without anchor, unless our dealer is home.
plum this city:
its detritus contains artefacts suitable for reimagining ourselves
as anything other than *other.*

ii.

butterflies in stomach's well.
they emerge when our dealer responds, says:
yes, a veil
... come.
glass shards shall Picasso our face, world.
transparent scales slant.
light colours in the colourless lines.
we become a flurry.

iii.

credit can feed.
if it doesn't, we try emotional bulimia
& throw up over ourselves to induce sympathy.
on occasion it works
... unlike us.

iv.

our skin is tattooed, is a nexus of giving in:
this bliss is a perpetual mess.
micromanage torment with anguish.
gang up against reluctance.
you are blasphemy in the city.

v.

admit it: we've always prided ourselves on being *other.*
exclusion pertains to an absence:
now that is something we can follow.
space:
we are it.
we are constrained by a liberty of our own creation.

vi.

street:
it's where we meet.
we are bleak, freaks.
we bang-on.
we stink of this: aesthetics of cold sweat.
how we release midnight madness:
it begins as whisper.
this dark rapture a choir, articulating pain city commissions with glass spires.
in our human hearts, unfed on method, we make ourselves thin.
we transform into something that scares you.
that scares us too.

vii.

go wrong all night long.
sing a rough song.
put your withered being in your throat.
hear how it amplifies the croak.
blood nooks your arm.
this, a liturgy of self-harm.

viii.

"a river runs through all of this"
swamps beneath shit & piss.
calls outs, tugs our unblinking eye.
pale in sunlight:
see blood sump movement.
if only we were liquid:
then we could pour self over & through bitumen, pavement.

ix.

who views us?
they do:
the people who you long to vacate the aching shapes of glass & steel.
like we have vacated the citadel of our self.
when we stop to articulate our need in vagrant streets, we are babel.
from their remnants, we build, devour.

x.

soiled mattresses seed inner city curbs.
they call to loll & fuck
at regular intervals.

xi.

concentration should be avoided at all costs.
instead, get lost:
it is cheaper & much more fun.
the sun is a circle we hide from.
do not travel here after three am:
the streets accost, ganking as they want.
walk until corn grows beneath feet:
let earth reclaim this city.
look for a grave to own.

xii.

a minus of degrees:
mighty tundra, come.
we summon you through crack pipe's chemical dew.
gather in the bulb of the world.
we heat to inhale.

in order to implode, just blow.

xiii.

sweat leads to sweat:
money lent is money burnt.
we come, we sew.
our accounts are hollow:
we debit & bleed red.

xiv.

even the animals hate us.

familiar is only an ache.

xv.

we adore living these haunts.
we are a flaw, disappear into walls.
see us mould.

xvi.

after half past four, streets are swept clean, mechanically.
we act nonchalant beside their hiss & spray, spit words over activity.
this is the beginning of night's end:
from here, vehicles swerve fluent verb.
cars park to carpark globe:
a multistorey boom gate, industrial.
exhausted, fumes consume dawn as traffic peaks, ecstatic at running late.
we arrive at a destination & day takes us away to sleep, embarrassed to do so.
reluctant, we give in, as if driven.
just walk around us without indication.

xvii.

time is a mug.
outside the cathedral, we thug the living shit out of it.
it possesses a face where feet & fists we place.
we steal seconds & mechanisms & whoop.
but time can wait, calculate, plot revenge.
administration occurs as object of governance:
if ever we are stopped, our actions warrant a rest.
inside a cell, long blue arms hold us
as we dangle.

xviii.

we are fixture.
we burn electrical.
if we die now, nobody will know

at least that's what people spit, under their breath.

xix.

in desperation we drink the water used to filter our meth pipe.
in three days' time, we'll sleep.
when we awaken, we shall return to our childhood home.
here, we will forage for value.
then sell it.
if we make it out of this alive, we can buy it all back.
a loan is not committing a crime.
is it?

xx.

inject the word of god into blood.
hear her speak.
how she carries us.
praise be, for she is holy:
so are the arteries this worship hurts.
when all the veins in our arms & legs are murdered
she will go for the jugular.

xxi.

we *are the walking dead.*
hunger logic, death wish meds.
to persist, we insist this is community service:
highlight a modern blight by trailing city's life so no one else has to.
how noble.
give thanks.

xxii.

we stink of amphets,
fear,
The Fright.

THE SLEEP DEPRIVATION DIARIES

Of course, it's hard to tell how much of this is fiction, or even whether all of it is.

– Chris Fleming, *On Drugs*

prayer for the parents of every addict

ahem

meat emanate
that heat
him, imp
aim pin
inmate, hit it
animate anthem
pant aphanite
eat ten het men
attain mania
methane mane
heap teeth
ante mint
theme thin
team tinea tin
name paean   paint Pan
patient
patinae, pain, maim

methamphetamine, emit hate
meme at heathen me:
i   am   them:
mime; manatee; mine; meanie;
a meth matinee;
the pi hi eaten meatpie;
pieman; hitmen; apeman; titmen;
an anime heap, anti-neat;
inept nap;
hath tine tip.

pa
ma
mama
tempt teatime
nip amphetamine neap
tame pent pen
tie thine time titan
then theta tap

ai

amen

The Sleep Deprivation Diaries

Day 1.

? am i imaginary.

XX believes so ~~tells me as such~~.
when her lover leaves
she summons me from across the mighty tundra. i appear ~~banishment is never forever~~ as a hologram: gems are made from this, because jewels are her best friend ~~as are the imaginary versions of herself~~. from memory, i can remember how to do this, vaguely. *you may have one*. i try to remember ~~who i was & what that person would have done instead~~ but these rules, these rules we make up.

someone just played shop. i made her happy. ~~but not with love~~. with love, i buy XX odd little thoughts from the curios i find attractive. i am the fake. i am cold inside. *Cryongenic Joan*, somebody calls out, but not at me.

someone rings.
i use my XX voice.
the entire phone call.
he loves my new mood. but i'm not her.
i'm me faking her with expert precision.
we love a little fakery.
he asks if i'm wearing my fuck-me-boots.
i lie & say *yes, of course dear, now what the fuck do you want.*

i call her XX because i can't remember her name.
for legal reasons.

Day 2.

XY is in attendance the whole time. we make our own vends. he too is a small business owner: he teaches me how to be my own boss. XY has big plans. bigger hands. the biggest rock we seek out. together, we shoot the night and i become a hologram: it's showtime.

i wear a ship captain's hat
& a rusty chain that jangles, as if nerves,
wrapped around my throat. i'd say it was a metaphor
but i dunno what they are right now.
? maybe the ceiling does ?
XY reaches out
– but not in the way i want –
to pull me back down before i float off.

do i make you happy XX. she makes me roll. we roll like this. ~~i get lost, drive around the block~~. i pull in to Tartarus, barren save for oil stain salted concrete. someone shines a torch in my face. *there's a light / over at the Frankenstein place*. i memorise the map home. my heart is a rust bucket, rattling. i pray to a god who does not love me anymore.

in the politics of this, i am the pet you cannot deny. we are addicts. XX has so much junk. whack: i'll hit you across the back of the head whenever i want. *here, take this. it's the gold coin for the ferryman*. XY will field all existential engineering enquires. do you steal. & is it theft. or are you merely saving others from it… as if doing community service. ganking stole the space back. we klept. siphon from the top. cut will grip to the side of the bag & besides
there isn't any in the house.

this compendium of secrets
& insider tip bits
has to be compiled
in snatched fragments
because so much literally happens
see: here i am off on another adventure
before it has time to happen. i am the fake.
i am a hologram:
a kate moss rolling stone i am the fake.
gathering out of a mcqueen

mist & ether   i am the fake.

burning in the fireplace.

we are addicts. an addict adds & subtracts. we don't do math: we do meth. belligerence & brilliance. she collects so much junk that she could fill a fleet to ferry their ware down a river of sticks. the fake i am. & for this she loves me. even if i'm trouble.

Day 3.

XX sleeps. but i can't remember how to.

someone texts & XY says *yes, tell them to come round, honest... you won't regret it.* what they show us looks as though it had been ripped from scree. it rips us instead. i grip the furniture for support. oscillation
occurs. busted: it's when your eyes
escalate into orgasm, jeering from side to side.

i am the fake imaginary man as an imaginary woman.

i come down feeling like milk
curdled.
cuddled.
muddled.
turtle.

there is a jungle gym in my bedroom.
not that i ever sleep that much *down the river of nights dreaming.*
XX does: she does marathons.
of bunting.
~~of hunting the sleeping snark~~. we run out & roll. roll with us.

there's a light / even in the darkest night. we burn candles. both ends. wax lyrical. there is no point to this, except pointing itself. we pinprick & stitch, puff & cloud. i can feel the scar tissue succumb to the itch. push & jackback. blood is a plume. i dance electronic. i am the fake XX, imaginary of the real. i talk just as much. XX owns so much, but in unison, XY & i exclaim *but she knows exactly where everything is.*

& yet, between us, her stash is disappearing.

Day 4.

nomenclate. we name things to make sense of what we have. & she really has so much.

things i have found include:

a year book from Denton High; magenta lips; science fiction novellas; ~~mystical cinema brain~~; rice enthused with vowels that *give you the eye & then panic*; ~~a chewing hospital~~; a water gun; newspaper hats; a flashlight; *velvet darkness*; a brochure for The Oakley Court Hotel in England;

watches, touched by Dali, warped; ~~possible collapsed meds~~; tinned curry; corsets; rubber gloves; beakers & a Bunsen burner; a liquid rainbow flag; ~~my hands are disappearing~~; confetti for celebrating creation; a noisemaker, silenced; ~~be quiet as you search, lest she hear you~~; gold hotpants, just like those worn by Kylie; a sword; a ruler with the name *Damocles* painted on it; *the start of a pretty big downer;* ~~this is the point of no turning back~~;

a desk calendar, only 7 days long, *weighing 98 pounds*; free weights with bows on them; *raw eggs*; ~~49 used syringes, all capped~~; a potato sack; saxophone reeds; vintage Harley helmet; an axe; a recipe for meatloaf, even though no one eats; ~~you know all the lyrics~~;

surveillance cameras; a feather boa; ~~a system that produces abuse & binging~~; a vintage telephone; a lost song; a deleted scene *to make the break*; ~~cut your hand on broken imagery~~; toilet paper, hoarded in case of pandemic; old toast; ~~red shoes that you should never have put on, because now you can't stop dancing, oh harbinger of small disaster~~; Eddie's teddy; exercise gear *to build your thighs up*; hot dogs; rose coloured glasses; pills to *take this dream away*; fishnet stockings; a motto to live by; a transit beam; diamonds & spades; *cards for sorrow, cards for pain:*

instructions on how to turn a house into a space ship; super hero costumes; *taste the flesh / not yet deceased*; ~~& the smoke machine turns on, pours dry ice across the backroom where all of this is displaced, & you, crawling mountains of muck as you search for~~

~~meaning~~; an insect; bloody knees; a key to Richard O'Brien's office desk;
& that's just for starters....

XY says *this isn't the movies,*
you can stop singing to yourself

? can he tell i am unravelling ?

after all this cataloguing
i still do not sleep.

Day 5.

. i cower inside the house: *the sun and light come streaming*, have woken the neighbours up. i have to travel to the shops. ~~people are germs~~. XX wants smokes. i slip out the back gate, up laneway. ~~slowly into this never-life~~. surreptitious. The Night Men did just this. except their hands, not their head or mouth, were the only things dripping with shit.

if you could see me
you'd shudder
: i am ghost other
grey fringe of slobber
drying at the corner of
the mouth
ranting at the day & night

. from out the corner of my sight
~~paranoia~~
~~paranoia~~
~~paranoia~~
shadow people wave hello

. see now how conversations
drop
. crash clatter bang into every
. can't remember where i
. so easily distracted by
. sleep will claim us
. sleep will claim
. sleep will
. sleep *flow morphia slow*

. don't come, not just yet. ~~profit to the street~~ .

~~hyperactivity is confusion smoking~~. you got any rock cod?
got some lovely crack mackerel ~~a cartel of lead consumption~~.
~~shared days in use~~.
scoop out and scoop back violent fables. ~~that of nosebleeds,~~
~~depression & tweak laboratories~~. ~~a crystal of craving~~ .

~~makeup tooth: the tremor in a tundra~~. every white space here is
something you shouldn't know

... we do stupid things when we're this high
for this long
, XX says, shaking her head
: there is so much missing from her
& it has my fingerprints all over it

. like getting higher *again*
, XY says & i blush
chewing the inside of
my mouth.

Day 6.

————————there comes clarity
sublime & silent after this rocky horror, this picture show:
XX sends me home

my body a seared liquid
prompting a finality in the hope of happier symptoms
conjures instead a still
lab stimulant versus bathtub damage
an attention-deficient of the binge

me: a house, a mouth, spewing nonsense no cents
just to make XY laugh
touch me affectionately because all i want is that
paranoia a permafrost in the few cells remaining, a remnant
a reward, a clot
i hide so many crystals
inside this flesh, create
the nervous will & blue risk of the rush
as blood refrains inextremis

see how i mutilate this body
abysmal & artisanal

see how the narrative has collapsed
from exhaustion
as if this were an inner-monologue

higher, the system strokes
this disease a drug and needle
sleep compiling credits

the controlled can last
but none of us can control this

in The Before, we were all
such nice people

but this structure causes a
psychotic function: how the white colonises terra with terror

i was somebody when i began
but now i am no thing as if imaginary
i imagine myself vanishing
as
a stain grows across this

i will be back in a few days to do this all again——————

Day 7.

Space of absent-head, elongated place where dreams
lack but cells knot themselves back together as
errors undo into an electrical soothe of circuitry.
esemplastic equation, solidify within
pockmarked skin: wake up   real again.

songs for the ordinary mass

i. climacus

speeding stopped
behind line white

hot is the colour
on top. tyres vomit &

rubber wafts. reed
high note crescendo

, blows blow a
concerto ready to oboe

forth. the engine revs
. foot is lead

. the destination is needed
, urgently plumes

. the patience is
dead. people cross lights

super slow, shuffle, fist
cradles horn, expectant of

complete traffic system
collapsing in on itself, as if

physics so easily torments
. swear to gods *I've gotten*

every fucking red light
tonight as though they care

. when it comes, the punch will
draw blood, either from the

head or what the hurtle stops
.

ii. porrectus

salvation alms
: loaves & 2wo

tuna tins. 3hree
cut out coupon kids

buy the bare
essentials, the basic

need. they feed
instead on crystal

, tweak like
sacrificial

lambs
bleat

, smell like Shabu fugues
. method has madness

. *wanna buy some*
rock

?cut with Epsom for
extra rush

.

iii. clivis

fuck man
. in vein they

miss living a
dreary & normal

abscess. squatting, these
diuretics do a diorama in

night lanes, with
drama. what little is

eaten is breaking is
cheeked bone. needing a

little
tenderness

they
croon their spoon &

pin the whole of
oblivion

iv. punctum

side alley, shooting
gallery, luck luck

junk
& muck

. culture swims with
little fish. pure pops

up, an import hounding
. this far left of null

& void the white
horse hits hard

, helps them drop
out the lot. *oh my*

god…! somebody
call an ambulance

. please! somebody
?! call triple

fucking zero
. people give berth

, watch without
looking at the

human car crash of
another overdose

. the wails inevitably
become those of

paramedics driving the
wrong way up roads

.

The Disappearing

Everything not saved will be lost.
– Nintendo 'Quit Screen' message

Every dose is a dance with death.

Take yourself to the edge.

They will say it is accidental: there is no box to tick for deathwish.

If you let go, you might never find your way back.

How you revel in the harm of this ongoing matter.

When you awake, you are convulsing.

On a stretcher, you are stretching thin.

We're losing them.

Now you are moving through the metal rods of the bed.

You ascend.

Flesh is for the unbuckling.

How, to get up there, you have to float.

Cathedral of your body, elope.

Turn back, see how small I have become.

As if I am insignificance.

puppy's howl

in your absence i am ghost dog
howl hollow bark, this haunting fidgets the edge
shivers are for the cold : instead, i tremble

like a puppy i run head first
into traffic, paws fall as cars
chicken accident

they do not spirit me: i am
too consumed, eyes all moon

each trip you take deadens me awake

that's why i run away

into black sprawl, sniffing for the blanket of your snore

flee(t)

fox, run, fox on: the farmer's
gun is sun, cracks an opera
across paddock, how it
follows you home, echoing

faster, red bolt of bush fur,
whirr creek on muddy paw,
your bloody roar all
tongue dry from panting

vulpine firestorm, contour
horizon's blue, emit smoke
whimpers, a plume as
this tale blazes behind you.

CLEAN

I used to think it was like a light bulb, life,
dangling in the chest, asking to be switched on.

But it's not the light that's ever in question,
rather, what's your brilliant, glaring wattage?

– Ada Limón, *The Other Wish*

Clean

i.

After one day, you still haven't slept. Wonder what you're doing with yourself. Energy grates. Grinding makes you deaf. Remember, all poetry begins with a decision, either to be read or to be written. You are a poem: from this, an epic. Getting clean begins with cleaning, so clean. Dispose of all sharp things responsibly. Replace with forgiveness.

ii.

After four days, sleep has come. Hard. The majority of it you spent unconscious: so deep you left an indent on the other side of the mattress. Hypnos was glad you finally stopped by, took the time to realign, reshape landscape. Let the crush of blanket be mortar, a foundation to vanquish. Allow ruby slippers to be stolen. Do not chase after them: red shoes make you dance until you're dead. Instead, remain buried. You shall arise, anew, from this grave, adorned in resilience, dew.

iii.

After one week you still feel like shit. This is your own fault. Please note: this is not an excuse to return to what you learnt by rote. Instead, drag yourself though the days. Fill veins with nutrients. The stink of chemical: out, seep. If all else fails, sleep: you're getting really good at it.

iv.

After three weeks, your dealer texts you. They wanna make sure you haven't died. Do not reply: they only concern themselves with your coin. And addiction. Theirs is one of misery capitalism. If necessary, drink coffee to give yourself a kick. Those flashes of fun that burn in your brain? They shall haunt you for as long you travel down this road. Remind yourself that these desires, they are dying: let them. Sometimes death is slow. And painful.

v.

After five weeks that money in your pocket shall yearn to be spent. Buy yourself books. Or a new look. Or more food to fill up the aching behind ribs. Replace all the things that crystal took.

vi.

After two months the colour returns to the world, your cheeks. You are filling out your form as if ticking boxes. For reassurance, all progress is progress. If your dealer calls, block them. You are touching sun. Reward yourself with poems. Become addicted to something other than destruction.

vii.

After four months you will feel human. It is a path of calendar. The mark on your arm has lost that colour, is no longer bruised. It is a reminder. Take each day in your arms. Slow hug that lasts 24 hours. Be proud of small accomplishments, like looking at yourself in the mirror without flinching. Muscle is taut. You, un-gaunt. Make tea. Smile softly.

viii.

Pink cloud an apostrophe in sentence, lifting. Five months on. Heady moments of recollection: the body has memory, remembers maelstrom. Nature is speaking clearer. Stones sing as they once did. Clear space inside yourself: there is grief, encroaching. Your mother will forgive you. The city will too. Walk with both of them. Watch as age takes hold. Gain more weight: shame is such a heavy, useless emotion.

ix.

After six months you will still be haunted. But at least you're clean.

In Somnolence

i.

Orpheus mourns the loss. All things here are rectangular: this bed; this pillow; this poem. You are a crescent moon: you shall not set yet. You'd count sheep but you're concerned with the ethics of farming livestock. So you count sirens. Ponder urban crime rates. How soil unlearns a pattern when tilled too much. Be torn apart by this hunger of night. You toss. You turn. If you had a clock, you'd be the tick. Sucking, the minutes yearn.

ii.

Sleep of theta; sleep of data; sleep of jolt; sleep of the low rapid volt; sleep of Strauss; sleep of mouth; sleep of speaking secrets out; sleep of walking; sleep of fire; sleep of water; sleeping fish, we do retire; sleep of poppy; sleep of tea; sleep of horn and ivory; sleep of Hypnos; sleep of Tutu; sleep of Baku, come eat my dream; sleep of grief; sleep of wreath; sleep done nightly 'tween paper sheets; sleep of fall; sleep of thrall; sleep alarmed by morning call; sleep of sleep; sleep so deep, but not the sleep our souls to keep.

iii.

When did you and Morpheus become such good friends? The bed fellows, sleep follows. A coffin is a rectangle too. Made from cotton. Cling of earth, hum: R.E.M. mends. Cells knot. Dreams unclot. You are slow decay: this rot is healing. Is inevitable, like tomorrow. Grow crops behind eyelid: Viper's Bowstring; Peace Lily; Valerian; French Lavender; Devil's Ivy. When you splay your arms apart, it is as if you are a scarecrow, awaiting resurrection. Sleep has come, carrion.

a brief language of crow

at dawn, crows chew colloquial news, how
they eat apple to the core, adore bin day,
scavenging horizon, prying off garbage lids.

a ghost i met once said *watch what all those*
murders do: they are on to me, on to you.
these funerals are a clamour: black becomes the

colour of how a beak can glamour. corvine
law sees them tearing down walls, clattering
claws on gutters, one blue eye watching you,

the other sky, blinking in half-light. these would
be writing desks, they swoop now: the magpies
bark & scowl. i heard that down south, the crows

even dig out meth discarded in petrol station
trash cans, much to the amusement of watching
cops.

Snowy (An Obituary)

In the real world, we exist. A multiplicity, present. A gift as brilliant as snowfall before green swallows whole. You did not know this in high school: that world was just gym-short thoughts, sideway looks and so much straining to be loved. But right there, on TV, emerged teenage visibility: Heath Ledger as Snowy in *Sweat*, with impossible blonde curls, eyes so heavy, & those legs – the snow inside me melted.

Then, eventually, you. Years later, just as impossible, curled around my head, heart caught between the pinch & frostbite. You, in my bed: your skin a snowfall, whispering the world into oblivion.

Snow: I remember snow fondly, all six foot drifts and frozen toes, a giant white pillow. I remember you fondly as I remember snow: just as breathtaking; just as cold; just as temporary. Just as temporary

as snow on the heath.

kangaroo paw

blood beats red, thumps in elation, dread.
how, as an immigrant, my ears rang
with this land, sang exodus on arrival.

that time, in the cemetery near my house,
as a kid, we heard a tattoo of paw drumming
floor as though knocking from the dead.

"kangaroos," somebody said.

we were ghosts among ghosts, white as moonlight.

& now, years later, i marvel at how points
of departure are a tone drumming up through bones.

& still kangaroo paws trill with gesture.

but now they beckon us toward them.

How Joy Arises

What are eyelids if not parentheses. Open them. Outside, white cockatoos squall, call magpies to bring their maps as crows crackle on the industry of hymn. The puncture of Venus is healing into blue as a body, celestial, rises. Stretch. Step out of bed: wooden cradle; ship; see how sand collects at the corners. Sheets lapping. Coffee splutters through the grind of a machine. Between ankles, cat threads fur, to mewl and meal. Open phone. Let news spool into view. Some will be the kind you really ought to sit down for: how knees know when to buckle. Acknowledge this, let go. Because amid it all there is hope. Give gratitude, send love, trust. With tender hands we should use a word like *prayer*, and we have. Yes, it is another day… like so many you have lived before. But you are here, now.

Maternal Memories

// you can hear it in her voice / accent speaks of other world / other home / India existing nearly a century ago / tripping vowels / hardening consonants into a continent of post-verbal idiolect / the kind that resides in bones / and blood / when my mother swears, she does so in Hindi / words so blue that, if i said them to you now, my tongue would fall out / but in the kitchen, when the tricks of a traditional dish slip comprehension, these curses are verses / chime off pots and pans / cutlery / dinner plans / climb from her throat as sharp as spice sprinkled from fingers, wrinkled / biting with many blessings / a sting, vindaloo / boil rice / softening to become base / in the backyard, she grows mango / from seed / a deed that has taken over a decade to achieve but, here they are now / how they entertain us / ripe skin unbuckling to suckle on / she trades these with an Indian lady around the corner / their food economy an algorithm that kicks in the moment it passes 9am / phone rings / son sent gathering / collects dishes that speak of shared motherland / a place, to me, unknown / but one i can taste in the chaat masala and rosewater / the saffron and ghee / colliding into me / a vegan onslaught that makes my body brim / and i turn to Google to give me approximation of what their land looks like / ask *Mt Abu, where are you?* / discover how many corners a train took before it crested border / the chromaticity of earth / aroma of dirt / fill it all in with tales / memory from her, living / how Partition saw women killed before her eyes / in her ears, still, their cries / how her father would find animals, frail / exhale whispering that saw them grow, heal / snake / raven / chipmunk / calf / crow / all manner of creature he would craft back to health / well is a well / a skill passed down / one that lives in my mother / sees me trying to quell a mastery over this beast, the poem / she tells me of her siblings fighting over clothes, eyes afire / her the youngest of them all / watching with a smile while eating dhal / and this other world, in my bones, i know i can find you / if only over oceans i can travel / but until then i ask her, often, to drown me in her memories / hoping, one day, when she is gone / i am able to remember them / write them down / fill in the spaces between here and that world / the one that wrapped this mythology around her / as girl //

Reworking slurs I was called from when I was using

after Luka Buchanan

TAKE A LOOK AT THIS (augment of wind-flower)

FUCK MATE WHEN DID YOU LAST (swim not knowing up)

(take this poem home) & GET CLEAN, YA MUTT

DIE (trying to say every thought at once, once again)

THIEVING (a god particle)

(i am in love with the high places) OF THE EARTH

ALL YOU JUNKIES DESERVE (compassion & a warm bed)

DO US ALL A FAVOUR AND (graft saplings / to rock face / at the edges /
of the compass)

(hooves make for comfortable shoes) & KEEP ON WALKING

BLOODY (kitchen cupboards / full with expiration dates)

WHAT HAVE YOU DONE TO (keep it together)

(flatten the earth into four corners again) OUT OF MY HOUSE

YOU STINK OF (corpse flower breath)

WHY DON'T YOU JUST (let it crawl out of your head)

(a ghost, mechanical) IS GONNA BE A DRUG ADDICT

YOU CAN'T LIVE UNDER MY ROOF IF YOU (scrape a nebula of life
across the wet barrel night)

This Is Not A Manifesto

Because I am still manifesting. At the age of 42, my gender identity is more fluid than ever. Inside, I am aqueous. Outside, I do not know which pronouns best suit me: been using *he* and *him* for so long I wonder if they are who I am. Or who I was. Who was I again? When I was 10, I told my mother I was gay: at the time, it was the only word I knew for *other.* From there, my being flowed from bi to queer to non-binary masc. This body is a mask, is drag. Dress up every day. Have learnt the heteronormative performative walk of men who think the world owes them something. Call on such a strut whenever I have to slip through the streets at night, appear as if I don't give a fuck, even though it makes me dysphoric. There are days the testosterone surges and these urges remind me of what it means to be *toxic.* I am learning to be brave again: men have bashed me for being "too" feminine. Appropriate active-wear vacant stares of "men" going nowhere. I am learning to be brave again, be myself. Pray for the day that the dress declares itself androgynous. And all other garments follow suit. Pockets abound. Buttons refuse to conform to preordained societal gender norms. High heels become the free toy with every Happy Meal. My hope is to make the veil a socially acceptable accessory that you can wear in the roughest suburb. But why should we hide who we are? My friend jokes, tells me to use *tHEy* and *tHEm* as my pronouns. I do not laugh: there are days when even using a capital *I* feels like taking up too much space. I am learning to be brave again, because I am still manifesting. One day, write a manifesto about this. Until then, weep at the bravery of those who are younger, so much more certain of how to speak the uncertain. And, for now, I shall identify as *human*, because it is the only word I know for *other*.

forty-nine mobile phones

for Pulse, Orlando (June 12th, 2016)

what is the sound of a kiss between a man & a man if
your worldview
perverts you
from seeing all the homely people, where do
they all come from...?

here, Eleanor Rigby
is a drag queen; beetles
bump beneath skin
as bones bounce in ecstasy; & Orlando is
a woman who
was once a man who
is now a woman
again.

in musical theatre
it is perfectly the norm
for men to
dance, a chorus line form:
the same can happen in a
nightclub, so come
seek sanctuary:
after all, closets
are for lions, witches & wardrobes.

but him?
- that one
whose name
now gives him power
beyond the grave
& his legacy
already stains rainbows –
he's out to bang the cocked gun
of being human
& all the hate that can bring....

Hot Damn; A Screaming Orgasm; Redheaded Slut; Slippery Nipple; Sex On The Beach; Birthday Cake; Prairie Oyster; Rumple Minze; An Ice Luge; Goldchlager; Jagermeister; Kamikaze; Mind Eraser; Bombs; The Three Toed Sloth; Boilermaker; Fireball; Flaming Lamborghini; Chartreuse; Schnapps; Absinthe; Cock Sucking Cowboy; Clit Licking Cowgirl:

these
are the only shots that should
be heard
ringing out
in a nightclub!

what is the sound
of a kiss
between their death
& your living?

forty-nine mobile phones
call out
in unison....

She Knows No Spell To Quell A Tsunami

for The Global Climate Strike, Friday September 20th 2019

i.

Mother learnt magick on the picket line.

Curses were verses scratched into car doors using iron nails from shipwrecks: Europa; Alkimos; Cervantes.

How she would paint sigil onto placard.

Superglue was always blessed.

As were chains, padlocks, causes.

They'd walk out into a sacred circle, bless that space, a glimmer across asphalt.

Then, they would begin chanting.

ii.

Mother taught me semantics are a form of magick.

Incantations are merely emphasis, inflection.

Detection is a difference between words like *queer!* and queer: how spit can be soft on a
tongue.

How *strike* once meant surrender.

A ship, captured, dropping sails in submission.

Used by colliers on the Thames: a stoppage to the flow.

Sailors; lightermen; coal-heavers; glass-grinders: fourteen thousand of them marching toward Westminster.

All for fair pay.

But now, a strike is 1.4 million schoolkids walking out of class to reduce fossil fuels and the fossils who advocate for them.

Dinosaurs thought they had time too.

A mass of angry children will wake up the entire world.

Stop denying the Earth is dying.

This September's strike: there will be more, us.

This deteriorating Earth: see how we are weathering.

Us, bound in movement, our destination a matter of degrees.

Mother says *our mouths curve to find new words in words, spelt exactly as they were, always have been.*

iii.

Mother worries: she knows no spell to quell a tsunami, to calm a climate.

How easily a man can change his mind... or be made to think he has, she says, *but a planet?*

She scours texts, converses with what is left: of her coven; of her grimoire; of the white-knot ocean's top, pockmarked with plastic.

Klimatångest is rife.

Eco-nihilism: a way of life.

But the youth stand up, walk out, protest & shout: wisdom quickening before a tide.

And now it is our turn: Ragnarok's lullaby is haunting.

Mother wants to help, but she – like Nature – is ancient: they both struggle with large crowds.

All she can do is offer me her hand.

When I ask if she wants to come with me to the Global Climate Strike, she refuses, says she will stay at home, watch the ocean.

In case the water begins to recede… then rise.

shout

after Allan Boyd's listen

extinction hunts : human blood is
on the beak & claw, feather & fur
snout & maw of every animal that
ever was. we raise slaughter like
sons

& daughters ask *why do the men*
with tiny white hands make such
plans : it's as if they wanna master
the art of environmental disaster &
leave

dry roads that erode the native bush
& mangrove, turn place into pasture
where humans travel faster & leave
nothing but asphalt. when they ask
if

this is all our fault we tell them how
we tried, how we watched crimes &
how we cried, how we sung to the
bulldozer, how we lost our composure
but

it was not enough. & still politicians
demanded land's blood. in the future
when climate change makes refugees
of us all, we'll be closer in degrees of
humanity

& still extinction shall hunt. it will
hear our songs of exhaustion, our
skin peeling, shaded from the sun,
smell all our plasma & run faster &
faster

: shout now or forever soil your peace.

Marri: Remembering Meelup Regional Park (An Obituary)

The forest breathes us in. We are chasing bush orchids. Kambarrang is brimming. Through a macro lens, petals bend, fill the screen. Blue; beard; duck. Your grin dazzles, blonde hair curling around my heart. We laugh. The forest smiles with us. Donkey; elbow; leek. Beyond the breadth of this, ocean swims. Here is the place of the moon rising. The forest sighs. As do I. You smile wide, engulf tree and leaf and trunk. Fire; slipper; sun. You say to me how love is a like a wildflower: a moment that recurs again and again when the conditions are perfect. As in how they are between us. Now. In this instance. Your kiss persists, travels through time, backward and forward. Fairy; helmet; hare. The forest knows that, in two years from now, we shall give up this connection. How, in four years time, I shall write these lines, and our love shall exist once more. For a moment. How sometimes a poem is just a memory, remembering. Hammer; rattle; babe-in-a-cradle. And I want to believe that love lasts forever, but the conditions fall apart, like us. This is why we take photographs. This is why we write from the heart. That is why I dance with you now, beneath the marri trees, in the hope that one day you would marry me. The forest breaths us out.

embodied

i. alopecia

in the shower, you remember:
hair is a limb
is language
once spooled sink full of thread
in clumps your body gave it, freely

stress reactor
heart was the factor that tore you bald
how you were just 19 years old & already
you couldn't make heads nor tails
of how to love a man

you never shall

ii. cavities

at the sink, you overthink:
the mouth is a hole, a portal
shovel in, spew out

acid of argument
of goading see how it rots

in the place where words sit
there is a perpetual trauma:
as kids we must loosen milk
teeth
give them to fairies

here, have a dollar
as if this is recompense

& now, your mouth is wrought:
inane, enamel clatters down the basin of your throat

how much dentin & pulp have you swallowed
to make your cheeks so damn hollow

iii. scar tissue

getting dressed, your body wears the scar as if address:
skin
around addiction
sing a song of suture
transgression is
a recitation repeating refrain
how the trace
remains because we like crossing over & through
the pull back & fold into

the rush, we convince ourselves, was worth this

the taint holds in the groove of a record
recording, deepens as body, in socket, revolves
loaded: without the track
a curtain is merely fabric, gathered, filled with holes & bullets

iv. psychic scar

on the way to therapy
wind has dislodged thin petals from
red flowering gum
so the road pools with blood

the horror is floral & subtle

in the therapist's office
you become dissociative flesh
& from above you can see your
interior's ecology

in circumflex & coronary
your arteries ignite, pulse:
here, you are doing the work

that pulls back
the blight to recommence
story, growth

healing is a magician's trick

when you find the fissure
that rips through your childhood home
& the shape of men that seethe there
plant *corymbia ficifolia*

know that hair will once more flow
new teeth can be purchased or borrowed
scars elate into mere trace
but your inner world will always need
tenderness

make appointment to return
same time next week

Soft Purple Warnings

Imagined Endings 1

In her mouth,
they gather,
fill our house.

The inference is missing:

                    dear mother,
what is a *thingy-me-bob*?

Perhaps a screwdriver, amethyst tip.
Tighten point to unslip. Or a pan.
Heather, collecting. Your thoughts
evaporate. Typically it is a hand,

reaching out. Grape with grip.
Hold on to this. But in Hindi
– the language she learnt
as child eighty years ago –
a prism imbues new Pantones.

In the garden, *aams* cause bough to bend.
Carotene blends into summer. We listen
to stories, sticky chinned.

When a blessing is required,
she tells me my *pooja* are
opalescent. Sacred gifts
shimmer to send out light.
Cleanse this space, us.

And our *mohabbat* are Valium.
Hold back the night.

But still the slippage comes.

Lesions plum tongue with ache,

pooling. There will come a day when we all
succumb, our iris incapable of comprehending
a room & those within it. The spoon will feed
conversation into her mouth. She will be body
unbuckling from shape of once-was,
how lilies will choke the vase: magenta is not
the colour of healing. But until then, I tell her:

Do not swallow these soft purple warnings.
They are not ber like the ones you grow.
Here is my hand, for holding: do not let go.

Red Flowering Gum

Home is a syllable in your heart. In order to speak it whole, clap it out: with glee; in ovation; as sarcastically as the Venus de Milo. Here, build new monuments from stone, adorn altars with flowers, the likes of which you have never known. But the Latin names are familiar, because back where you came from, somebody thought it'd be a good idea to teach a dead language to a blossoming mind. You now know 14 ways of saying you are bored in a tongue that nobody but biologists and doctors can understand. But you are not bored, not once you venture outside, feel sun in skin and discover *Corymbia ficifolia*. Firework fixed in blue. Firmament confetti bloom. Red flowering gum. You've only seen a tree bestowed with such beauty when bearing fruit. Or weighed down with the ornament of other seasons, consumed. But here, these trees spark strange light into sight. Cacophony of extravagance, brilliant in being unobtainable. That is until at school, when asking a fellow classmate what they are, they climb trunk and limb, begin showering red flowers down. And you, being a stranger learning how to spell this new home, you begin to clap.

on how to be a bird

surrender. give in. have faith that jumping,
submission first, will yield results: how

else can a fledgling be expected to leave a
nest? disappointment is grounding. success

is callus: you must catch every failure &
then let them go. from this process, learn to

treasure the shape of being victorious. bow
like a cello with a note reverberating in its

throat: this universe is the hand guiding you
to resonate. orchestrate conquest, not over

others, but the enemies within: doubt; doubt;
doubt. do not doubt yourself. see how, even

just then, it begets itself? there are those who
can assist you, bend twigs like mother bird

catches worm to dangle. achievement is
growing feathers: it happens, with time.

soon you too will have a cap full of plumes,
a head filled with wings, a horizon to fly into.

The Fisherman (An Obituary)

after William Dobell's painting Fisherman

In the gouache dark, moon teals the reeds. Rod a small god. Old testament. Plucks wrath in thrash of scales. But the fisherman prefers an apostle song. The names of so many men, swimming through him. Each time he catches a fish, he dubs it hymn, after a dead lover. Then releases it. If you teach a person to fish, they will never be lonely: river keeps good company. They sing to each other: feretory and octave. They both ache. Beyond the bend, the detritus of lives, left behind. Fisherman deepens knees. Into current, he breaths apology. His tears: a precursor to the diurnal. Out further, the ghosts of lovers. Abandoned beyond the tide that sticks, they look toward home: find nothing but fish. Him, marooned in blood, on the riverbank.

The Wilderness Steals My Mother's Voice

Imagined Endings 2

i.

Beside the dying pink of insulation bats, a microclimate: termites slaughter infrastructure, conjure borough. Out of beams they build a network of lightless galleries. Here, they debate the creation inherent in their destructive act. Anarchy begins this small, mounting. They speak in terms of alarm, direction, food source, a calling that pairs reproduction to the body, to the colony. Beneath, we hear the scritch of their politics. A mimicry of our own bones, fricative. Cracks filigree, feather ceiling. From her sickbed, my mother laughs at the symmetry of her own dying body and this house, about to fall in on itself. Her home groans: it is in on the joke.

ii.

Hooves plunder roof. Outside, a windhorse deluge. Mother refuses to cross over. *Not yet*, she says. Stubborn, her sweat wefts linen with outline of her shape. Her white hair a garland of salt lake. Beyond the roil, sunset nothing more than a shift. We descend into this. What is a storm if not the world saying *see, I too can break things*. This cannot be fixed: inside of her, infection exists. Colonised lungs. Each breath grasping. More thunder. Through plasterboard rift, dust stills, as if fireflies. The lights flicker. Inside my mother's chest there is a foal, trembling, pale. It looks just like me, at the edge of wilderness.

iii.

Elsewhere, other ecologies are collapsing. A koala clings to the top of a burnt blue-gum, searching for leaf and kin, her paws pink, blistering. In the artery of the Murray-Darling, cod and carp bloat as the current chokes for oxygen. Across two hot days, flying foxes amass grave. In an outcrop, a black-flanked rock wallaby gathers her offspring near: wind whimpers scent of surveyor. Serenade for end days: my mother's fever rambles from her throat. She tells me how every wrinkle across her body is a lineage, endangered or extinct. How, as a child, she wanted to make the world into an Ark. But the only wood she could craft was a coffin she called a home. Afloat on elegy, she struggles for breath. Elsewhere, other eulogies are being carved into earth and bone.

iv.

Pre-grief, press into me. How we harden before the shatter and gape. My mother sings gospel and hymn, rasping. She asks the termites to stop eating. They do not listen. Instead, a sound of something feral. I help my mother to her feet: she shivers, arctic. Yet her palms smoulder. As we step across the threshold, into the hallway, thunder is thrown from the clouds, through the ceiling. An eruption of plasterboard and beam as roof vomits on to her empty bed, covers us in dust. In the cacophony of cave-in, of termites screaming, of the wild wet outside entering our house, my mother begins to unravel. She becomes river; rubble; open cut mine; bleached reef's stubble on wind thrashed sand; an inferno; an inferno; an inferno. And, from above, a song leans in. It borrows my mother's voice and, from parched lips, sings:

you had
the whole
world
in your
hands...

create this city

... R & I R & I R & I Tower to watch Marilyn's lips kiss Boorloo's city skyline while she twirls her skirt a red shape balances by the QV1 turning step paused kangaroo's bouncing briefcase & pouches lamppost swans wrapped along outside casino on the other side of town a shouting man in The Cultural Centre where a Henry Moore used to be before it became an incense holder that's why it's now kept indoors past the pond once-were familiar pillars covered with posters outside PICA & its newly fuelled bar where poetry readings used to be diagonally across from adverbs written on a carpark's glass wall a glitter Christmas star over James Street crossroad corner coffee-house exhibiting art Arcane's funky windows no more now a collective collects on William as a Paper Mountain reaches sheath by sheath toward heaven black and white symmetry outside library always pointing north east west & south north east west & south north east west & south news about mapped tracks & central vacancy fourth floor looking out over traffic chasm swing around Central Park so unlike New York's with no muggers just a steel skyline structure trees in the other park lit up from beneath a monument to dead heroes a Bowie song a bough is sawn lengthy wood flower clock green lawn traffic sign our car plates say *this is a state of excitement* create this city as a rune it means initiation as a rune or secret matters as a rune it has an orange spot for emerging work geographically a lonely place bubbling on the west coast of this burning rock a rune is a rune is a rune is a rune is a rune back to the ground floor studio door a painter paints abstract shapes formed by watching buildings grow by being beside postmodern ruptures primarily steel always steel too much steel this land we steal yellow dust pushed up through the cracks thanks to the ants, who toil here as well...

Drawn From Life: A Brief Meditation on Time Travel

after Janet Carter's Drawn from Life *(2020)*

This poem is a temporal machine. Contains time and relative dimensions in space. Is a doctor, because poetry is medicine. Is shifting: hear the sound of an engine in your ears, thwomping.

Disclaimer: that could just be your blood.

Janet is sending you a Zoom invitation. Wants to chat. About the past, as a way to heal the future. This is what we do now: open windows on to other parts of the world, across time and space. We are talking. This is dialogue.

If the present is a fever dream, is that your teeth chattering, or do you just have a bad connection?

Conversation as a form of conservation. Archive as an arched life, how the spine touches finger's tip. We are not written yet. We are writing. With tongue. Through byte. Our screens, a tableau.

Somebody is speaking, but it's none of us. In fact, in every picture of our existence, we each have static mouths: this is intentional. Or we are leaning in far too close to the camera, all eyeball and hairline. This is also intentional. So who is speaking? You do not know. But the words belong to Douglas Crimp's *Mourning and Militancy*.

You are unfamiliar with this work. You Google it. In doing so, you come across a dodgy link. Click. Red banner warning: you are familiar with the flag of virus. Close window. Wonder if somebody has hacked your system. Stolen your identity. If they want to take your form, it's only fair they take all of you. Dear Identity Theft: to whom should we send the banking details for all of our outstanding student debt? To whom should we address this ever-present threat of violence?

You are watching Tony Kushner's *Angels in America*. It is May, 2016. The play is based in New York. You are at the State Theatre in Perth. The angels are tired: they have travelled approximately 18,700 ks and 25 years to be here, before you. At the climax of this production—spoilers, sweetie—the roof collapses on the stage. As bed ascends, wings are summoned. You are crying. Not because of this beautiful spectacle. But because you know how the story ends. So many lost. So many dead. So many surviving. The imprint on your community's collective unconsciousness.

Perth Train Station: pre-lockdown. Just. You have travelled 8 months into the past. You are wearing a mask, walking through Perth Traino. Those big screens that replaced all the classical music, they are beaming in images from Wuhan's Huoshenshan Hospital. The doctors are in hazmat suits. It reminds you of your childhood, back in England, mid-80s: doctors triple suited as they treat AIDS patients on TV. That grief you had no name for, back then... it surges, consumes Platform 5. Beneath your feet, a memory of swamp. This too, an imprint of unspeakable loss.

And, like that, you're back in the art gallery. On the screen, Janet is circling through screens. In her email folder you can see a booking for an Airbnb. The date, redacted. You wonder if she ever reached that destination, that room. Or if, like everything else right now, the reservation was cancelled. Travel feels speculative, fictitious. But somehow, time travel doesn't. Not here. Not now

You return to the exhibition at the exact moment you left: the salt on your cheek is a gift.

Ghost City (An Obituary)

Beneath ink and thumb, become. You told me how, when modelling for life drawing classes, you learnt to dissociate. So as to avoid arousal. Your body merely line and vector. Form rendered from angle. How an approximation of your being would appear across sheets. In each sketch, your eyes vacant. I soon realised that, when I wrote you into a poem, you would do the same thing: become object for an object, absent. In meaning and flesh. An architecture of avenue and throughway. Ghost city: so used to being a presence rather than actually present. Now, locked down, I sense you in these streets. Aching pin drops into the barrel of an unoccupied terrace. Crosswalk staccato echo. No gods in the cathedral. Or the spires attired with insignias of ecocide. What is a skyscraper if not a tombstone, each sheet of glass an obituary for another sacred site. Bird song fills the void where once fume coiled: each squall and call amplified off these walls. Their song travels further through the chasm. The virality of a tweet. On ledges they pack mud and twig. Air a language in roll and sweep. Wy-lah. Cree-cree. Clink-clink. Oooeee. The Derbal Yerrigan laps a water wing rhythm up across foreshore bitumen. You would have liked it here, now, this quarantined quarter. How we could only carve this much silence from out of night. The absence did not judge our hands, holding. Our kisses. Bodies hugging in six lane arteries, empty save for the endless light. The background fur of freeway a feral cat ready to pounce morning traffic. But with you gone, I try to draw you back in: ink beneath thumb. You do not come. Only your trace emerges as feather hymn: each avian swoop through these streets makes me think you are returning. But you do not: I am a ghost in a ghost city. This too will end.

ballad

we wear uniforms torn from Centrelink payments
always coming up short on rent, electrics, water corp:
blessed be the parents who house us.

we learn to wean ourselves
from off the night
the otherside of life.

how we navigated a city via back alleys
avoiding law as galahs swoop, squawk,
dodge cars, dusty sunset flock, lifting
our flightpath cold with passing stares
& kookaburra's midday laugh:
none of this matters anymore.

we have a grip on this monumental slip
– be it a disease or isolation or because of abuse
of even just because –
we toil to make words work:
therapy has worth.

admission hurts.

is the poem pulled through the nib of a pen
just as enlightening as the beading barrel's tip?

tattooed with need & needling
we signpost where not to go.

addict, retract: in place, awe for a new day.

marvel at flower
creaking concrete open
a bouquet amid grey.

this too is work.

Ingredients for Grief

Imagined Endings 3

Skin – *You have to make friends with gravity,* my mother says when I ask her how to cope with aging. Her body is a topographical map, spanning three continents and 86 years. She collects chiaroscuro as bruising: they fade into bushfire sunsets, lilac daybreaks. When I ask her what the collective noun for a wrinkle is, she replies: *I am.*

Hair – Moon gathers in her mane. I can judge the quality of her sleep by how big her hair is the next morning. It's either cloud or tempest. Selene's rain falls from my mother's scalp, collects in collarbone. She uses it to water the garden, grow mangoes. Each strand of hair that works loose, my mother uses to stitch the sun into the sky.

Bones – The big toe on my mother's left foot is broken, has been since I met her all these years ago. Yet she still walks as if a dancer. *You must always carry yourself with dignity,* she explains, *no matter the pain.* This is the secret she hides inside my body.

Death – It takes approximately two and a half hours for a body to burn when cremated. In her sleep, my mother will turn to smoke somewhere before dawn. I will begin that day in a pattern that repeats until my own smoke-filled dream envelops me. At her funeral, I shall read the eulogy, and will not cry. As promised.

Ritual – Once home, I will wear my mother's memory as a coat of ashes. I will sob. The tears shall grey. Rivulets soaking carpet. I will go outside, curl foetal, as if a seed, beneath her mango tree, the rain washing me clean. One day I will make friends with the weight of this.

Every Day

for Rebecca

i.

Footfall, territorial. Deeds carve up the way. You walk kerb, alley, pavement, greet magpies who push back, hymnal. Duet between themselves and lawn. Scrub to be dug. Little ones chatter, gather feathers across their form. You walk on. You want to bring back bobtail dominion, tree constellation, water of land, wet reed dance. To bring back granite tongue and those who have gone.

ii.

At home, flowers ablaut the bed: Geraldton wax, mauve daisies, white crocuses planted in the afterward. How they return. Keening, a raven feeds. Bottlebrush in beak, chest bloody, she ascends. Rosellas pare the fruit. When stars riot the night, you listen for boobook, heartbeat of this dark, wings alighting. Rapture of mice. You sleep and dream of her: a flat line trills to fill a hospital sky.

iii.

The next day, agapanthus: green apostrophe erupts into spray of speech. Jacaranda's call, purple across streets: the calendar returns to her, no longer in that room. This many years on, grass across her grave. Whenever you visit, you lie beside her. The breathing of each blade. A galah plume, discarded: her smile. If all time happens at the same time, then every day is eulogy. Suffering is a cycle of bird and bud and sun. Of meds and ash and want. You put on your shoes. Walk. There's a season just over the hill. Beneath a summer sun, a magpie warbles. Tears evaporate. The blossom is spilt.

granite

here, the irrefutable truth of stone:
hear a sentiment of what is meant

a kernel the shape of a rock
in your head, your voice, in you

speaking unspoken sediments
through one definitive audio statement

how a mountain can be built from this
how a pebble is the corner of a landscape

binding spell

sain yourself.

create sigil from your burden:
write down the name & number
of your dealers on a piece of paper,
then delete from your phone.

bind using black thread.

as you loop those who profit in loss
tell yourself
ritual is a form of recovery.

thank your addiction
for all you have learnt.

place in a jar
with vinegar & spit.

with wax, seal the lid.

bury this far away from where you live:
travel the distance an all-day ticket permits.
a crossroads, at midnight, will work. . .in a pinch.

or offer to the ocean:
ask for it to wash your feet
of all those paths that lead to scoring.

turn skin into unakite.

rosehip shall knit scars:
see tracks fade.

remember,
getting clean is a form of grief
so let go
of your own ghost:
a wake, every day.

The Morning Star

It turned out that here was a temple worth losing our wings for.
– your final words to me

light dying into light
last star, an offering
parades a way
knows sun will surge, urge
bird to fling benediction
from an egg

dogs wake
wander chiaroscuro, edge
lawn into suburb as nurses
return home to wash
prayer in dawn
& we untuck
ether, linen

fingers smear news
across screen as teeth,
brushed clean, undo
knot of glossolalia

& you, between epiphany
& epilogue, a eulogia
fading from breath:
your night visit ebbs
as the body up above
peels back wings,
enacts a daily ritual
of the world
becoming a world
again, one where you
                are gone

& the grass   weeps

Notes

The three quotes that appear at the beginning of each section from Bill Moran's *Oh God Get Out Get Out* (Write Bloody Publishing, 2017), Chris Fleming's *On Drugs* (Giramondo Publishing, 2019) and Ada Limón's *Bright Dead Things* (Corsair Poetry, 2015) respectively.

The Mourning Star – Alice Miller's quote from *Thou Shalt Not Be Aware: Society's Betrayal of the Child* (ed. Farrar, Straus and Giroux, 1998). This poem was originally published in Cordite.

him – This poem is a queer rewriting of The Lord's Prayer. Versions of this poem have appeared in the Fremantle Press anthologies *New Poets 1* (2009), *Fremantle Poets 3: Performance Poets* (2013) and *The Fremantle Press Anthology of Western Australian Poetry* (2017). It also appears in *Contemporary Australian Poetry* (Puncher & Wattmann, 2016).

It Begins With Burning (An Obituary) – Adapted from my short story *Us Boys Made From Smoke* which won the 2019 Wollongong Short Story Prize and was consequently published in Mascara Literary Review.

Homebake – The John Kinsella and McKenzie Wark quote appears in *<<speedfactory>>* (Fremantle Arts Centre Press, 2002). This poem was originally published in Four W 24.

inner pity poems – This sequence pays homage to John Kinsella's *Globe Hotel And Inner City Poems*. Such lines as 'You are blasphemy in the city' and 'are the walking dead' are direct quotes. Other lines such as 'our gravity has no centre', 'credit can feed', 'micromanage torment with anguish', 'we are constrained by a liberty of our own creation', 'we stink of this', 'go wrong all night long', 'concentration should be avoided at all costs', 'time is a mug', 'we are fixture… if we die now, nobody will know', 'inject the word of god into blood' are remixes of lines from Kinsella's poem. The line 'a river runs through all of this' appears on a paver as part of a memorial to Lenny Sexton at Perth Train Station. A previous version of this sequence was published by zine-maker The Department of Poetry.

The Sleep Deprivation Diaries – This sequence contains quotes from the soundtrack to *The Rocky Horror Picture Show* (1975). *Over at Frankenstein's Place* is quoted in Day 2, 3, 4 and 5. Other songs quoted in Day 4 include *Damn It Janet, The Sword of Damocles, I Can Make You A Man, Once In A While, Planet Schmanet / Wise Up Janet Weiss, Rose Tint My World, I'm Going Home* and *Super Heroes*. The majority of ephemera mentioned in Day 4 are a reference to *The Rocky Horror Picture Show* stage and film productions in some way.

songs for the ordinary mass – These four poems were previously published in *songs for the ordinary mass* (PressPress, 2009). This collection won the 2009 PressPress Chapbook Award, judged by Chris Mansell.

The Disappearing – A version of this quote appears in T. Michael Martin's *The End Games* (HarperCollins, 2014).

Reworking slurs I was called from when I was using – Inspired by Luka Buchanan's poem *Smile, Honey* (Wrong Dreams Press, 2017).

kangaroo paw, **Marri: Remembering Meelup Regional Park (An Obituary)** and **Red Flowering Gum** – These poems were commissioned by Red Room Poetry as part of *New Shoots*.

She Knows No Spell To Quell A Tsunami – Contains placard statements seen at the 2019 Global Climate Strike.

on how to be a bird – This poem was written as part of the 2018 Red Room Poetry Fellowship shortlisting and appears in *This Is How We Heal* (Hectic Measures Press, 2018).

The Fisherman (An Obituary) and **Drawn From Life: A Brief Meditation on Time Travel** – Both these poems were commissioned by Westerly Magazine and were written in response to artworks that appeared at *HERE&NOW20: Perfectly Queer*, held at Lawrence Wilson Art Gallery.

create this city – Earlier versions of this poem appear in *Interactive Geographies* (Poetry Etc, 1998) and *songs for the ordinary mass* (PressPress, 2009).

Acknowledgements

Poems in this collection have appeared in such anthologies as *Contemporary Australian Poetry, The Turnrow Anthology of Contemporary Australian Poetry, New Poets 1, Fremantle Poets 3: Performance Poets, The Fremantle Press Anthology of Western Australian Poetry, Sunlight of Ordinary Days: Twelve Poets of the Peter Cowan Writers Centre, Informalities, Spoken Word Perth 2014–2021, Recoil Eight, How Well You Walk Through Madness, Four W: New Writing, Interactive Geographies, The Cottonmouth Anthology, New Shoots* by Red Room Poetry, *Womb: Celebrating Mothers, Joy In The Morning* and *Hope For Whole: Poets Speak Up To Adani*. Poems in this collection have appeared in such publications as Island, Westerly, Australian Poetry Journal, Cordite, Rabbit, Stilts, Indigo, Creatrix, Alien Buddha Zine, Cottonmouth, Impossible Archetypes, Baby Teeth Journal, Enby Life, Enchanting Verses, Burning Jade Literary Magazine and online at Red Room Poetry. Some of these poems have won awards including Melbourne Poet Union's The Martin Downey Urban Realist Poetry Prize, The 2017 Glen Phillips Poetry Prize and The 2020 Poetica Christi Press Poetry Prize while others have placed in the 2018 Tom Collins National Poetry Prize, 2020 Alice Sinclair Memorial Writing Competition, Melbourne Poets Union 26th International Poetry Competition 2020 and 2021 Peter Cowan 600 Word Short Story Competition..

This collection has been made possible by countless residencies at places such as FAWWA's Mattie Furphy House, Peter Cowan Writers Centre and Vancouver Arts Centre. However, deepest gratitude goes to Katherine Susannah Prichard Writers Centre who included me in the 2019 Four Centres Fellowship, overseen by Fremantle Press and DLGSC. It was here that I was mentored by Les Wicks who helped shape the final sprint of writing and editing that this collection needed to reach this point.

To my publisher, Terri-ann White, thank you for launching my first chapbook in 2009 and for examining the previous performance incarnation of this work. Your honesty and passion has shaped my career, helped me reach this point – thank you!

Thank you to John Kinsella for seeing something in me back in 2006 and being a constant champion ever since. Your passion and wisdom has been so necessary and I appreciate all the space you, Tracy and Tim have ever given me.

Thank you for being a champion, Alan Fyfe: may our Gen X tales of the underworld transform 2022 and beyond. You seriously rock. As do you Maddie Godfrey: thank you for inspiring me and, without knowing it, helping me stay clean. To Joni, Saoirse, Biddle, Luka et al, your passion has been a constant flame, a source of hope, an inspiration. Allan and Tonja Boyd: thank you for being champions of mine since 1998 and for Perth Slam, a space where I can shine as my nerves tear me apart. To Kate Noske at Westerly: my sincerest gratitude for the space and energy you have shown me. And to the entire Perth poetry community: I love youse.

To Gary at WA Poets Inc: thank you for giving me a space where I can shine and build community and feel connected. I appreciate you and the committee immensely.

Thank you Red Room Poetry for seeing worth in me back in 2012 when I needed it most. You've been a constant source of magic. Tamryn Bennett, you rock. Thanks also David and Annie and everyone else: your passion has been a constant light.

Thanks to everyone who has ever given me a mic, a feature spot, a chance to appear at a Festival.

To Rowdy, thanks for listening to my poems. To Rig and La: thanks for the adventures. To Mumblz: rest in power.

To Malarkey Molasses Baudelaire, thanks for the comfort only a black cat can bring. You would have loved your new brothers, Beowulf and Bones.

Thank you Susannah for being the sibling that I needed.

And finally, to my mum – thanks for not kicking me out. Thanks for helping me get clean. Thanks for the laughter, the listening. I love you. Please don't read this book.

About Upswell

Upswell Publishing was established in 2021 by Terri-ann White as a not-for-profit press. A perceived gap in the market for distinctive literary works in fiction, poetry and narrative non-fiction was the motivation. In her years as a bookseller, writer and then publisher, Terri-ann has maintained a watch on literary books and the way they insinuate themselves into a cultural space and are then located within our literary and cultural inheritance. She is interested in making books to last: books with the potential to still be noticed, and noted, after decades and thus be ripe to influence new literary histories.

About this typeface

Book designer Becky Chilcott chose Foundry Origin not only as a strong, carefully considered, and dependable typeface, but also to honour her late friend and mentor, type designer Freda Sack, who oversaw the project. Designed by Freda's long-standing colleague, Stuart de Rozario, much like Upswell Publishing, Foundry Origin was created out of the desire to say something new.